Decodable Readers

Take-Home Blackline Masters

Grade 1, Volume 2

HOUGHTON MIFFLIN HARCOURT
School Publishers

Unit 4
Exploring Together

Contents

Go, Jones! 1A

So Much Fun 5A

June's Pictures 9A

My Mule, Duke 13A

At the Beach 17A

Who Will Teach Us? 21A

Plunk, Plunk 25A

The King's Song 29A

Ray Trains Dex 33A

Sweet Treats 37A

What Will We Do? 41A

Let's Eat 45A

It Was Snow Fun 49A

Boat Rides 53A

Fun with Gram 57A

Rex Knows 61A

Bedtime for Ray 65A

Pancake Ran 69A

A Springtime Rain 73A

Rosebud 77A

What can that big, big bone be?

10

Go, Jones!

by Trey Barney

illustrated by Linda Chesak-Liberace

Jones woke up. It was time to go, go, go! Jones will get Mike.

3

Mike had a bone.

"This bone is just for Jones," said Mike. "It is just for him."

Jones ran and got Mike. Mike dug and dug. So did Jones. Jones rode home with the big, big bone.

4

9

2A

Jones went home to get Mike
because the bone was so, so big.
Mike can help Jones dig it up.

Jones ran to get his bone. Jones
ran around and around. Then Jones
went to dig in the sand.

8

5

3A

Jones dug a big hole. What will go in this big hole? The bone that Mike gave Jones will go in it.

But look! A big, big bone is in the hole! It is such a big bone. Can Jones dig it up? Can Jones carry it?

6

7

4A

So Much Fun

by Rosarita Mencia
illustrated by Diana Schoenbrun

Jack had so much fun telling jokes!
So did Dan. So did Meg. So did Mo.

Before the sun rose, Jack got on
his bike. Jack rode and rode.

18

11

5A

Jack rode his bike to Dan's home.
Jack had a note for Dan. Jack put
tape on his note and stuck it up.

Dan, Meg, and Mo sat. Jack got
up. Jack spoke.
"I will tell a joke," said Jack.
"Let's hope it is funny," said Mo.

12

17

6A

Mo,

Go to Big Pond.
Get to the pond
before 9:00.

Bring snacks.

Jack

Dan woke up. Dan put on his robe. Dan got Jack's note. Then Dan went back in with his note.

13

16

Meg woke up. Meg put on her robe. Meg got Jack's note. Then Meg went back in with her note.

Mo woke up. Mo put on his robe. Mo got Jack's note. Then Mo went back in with his note.

14

15

8A

Bruce has a nice smile. Click.
June will show Bruce this picture.
June hopes Bruce will like it. Do you
think he will?

June's Pictures

by Jolene Odegaard

June likes to take pictures.
It is so much fun. Click, click, click.

June likes those little pigs.
She thinks the pigs are so cute!
Click, click, click.

The ducks have soft white plumes.
June likes ducks. Click, click, click.

20

25

10A

That mule is standing in a nice pose. June likes mules. Click, click, click.

Six cute dogs sit on steps. June likes dogs. Click, click, click.

24

21

11A

Cats are cute when they nap.
Cats doze a lot! June likes cats.
Click, click, click.

That gull stands on a pole.
June likes gulls and sand dunes.
Click, click, click.

22

23

My Mule, Duke

by Richard Stemple

illustrated by
Jackie Snider

June will play the flute. Duke likes June's tune. Duke will carry June home. Clip, clop, clop. Clip, clop, clop.

Duke is a big mule. Duke is a huge mule. Duke lets June ride on his back.

34

27

June is light. It is fun to sit on Duke's back. Duke will carry June home. They go clip, clop, clip, clop.

Duke likes June's tune. Duke gets up. Duke runs, clip, clop, clop, to June. Duke runs, clip, clop, clop, to the tune. Clip, clop, clip, clop.

28

33

14A

June will play a tune. June skips
to the tune. June hops to the tune.
Skip, hop, hop, skip, hop, hop.
June skips and hops to the tune.

32

No! No! Duke sits down! June
must go home. Get up! Be a good
mule, Duke. Get up! Duke just sits.

29

15A

What can June do? Duke just
sits. June must go home. Duke sits
still. Duke will not get up. June lets
Duke sit. June picks up the flute.

June can skip home. Skip, skip,
skip. June can hop home. Hop, hop,
hop. June can use the flute. June
makes a tune.

30

31

16A

At the Beach

by Elaine Sciofus
illustrated by David Sheldon

Then Pete has to go home. So do I. We had lots of fun. We will meet at the beach next week.

42

Pete is my best pal. We meet at the beach each week. We run and jump and yell. It's fun!

35

17A

Pete is six. So am I. Pete has a
green cap. My hat is green. We eat
sweet peaches at the beach. Yum,
yum, yum.

36

The sand beast is like an eel.
Maybe it's a snake! We run and
jump over it.

41

18A

We get a lot of wet sand. We make a neat sand beast.

Then we take a walk. Pete and I hunt for shells. We keep about five shells each.

40

37

19A

Then we sit by the sea. Pete gets his feet wet. My feet get wet, too. Splash, splash, splash! We don't go in the sea. It's fun to just get wet feet.

We dig holes. Dig, dig, dig! The sea runs in them. The holes fill up fast. We get wet sand.

Unit 4/Lesson 17/Selection 1

Who Will Teach Us?

by Forest Von Gront

Could you teach a friend? What could you teach?

Mom is teaching Beth about planting seeds. Beth makes holes. She plants seeds. Beth will water the seeds and see them grow.

50

43

21A

Miss Kim is teaching Lin a tune. Each week Lin meets with Miss Kim. Lin can read each note. She can play well.

Gramps is teaching Bill about fishing. Bill can hold his fishing pole just like Gramps. Gramps tells Bill to be still when fish are close.

44

49

Nell's mom is teaching Nell how to clean the car. Nell wipes it with a mitt. Nell will clean it so it shines.

Dad is teaching Sam how to swim. Dad is holding Sam while he kicks his feet. Sam will be so glad when he can swim.

48

45

23A

Bob likes to teach kids how to play this game. He meets with them each week. He teaches them to use their feet and kick.

Mom is teaching Reed and Pete how to bake. She will teach them to be safe. She is helping them place drops on the sheet.

46

47

24A

Plunk, Plunk

by Charles Barker

illustrated by Karen Stormer Brooks

"Helping you is fun," Jean tells Frank, "and it's fun to sing!"

"Ink-a-dink-a-thanks!" Frank sings.

Plunk, plunk! Drop, drop! Drops fall on Frank's cheek. What made those drops?

58

51

25A

The drops got big. Plunk, plunk. Did Frank see what made those drops? No, but Frank did see a hint.

52

"Which song will we sing?" Jean asks.

"Let's make up a song! Ink-a-dink-a-dee!" sings Frank. "Sing with me!"

57

"It was fun," Frank tells Jean.
"Will you help me rake? We can
sing as we rake. Rake, rake, rake.
Sing, sing, sing."

56

27A

A green hose is in the green
grass. Frank thinks it made the
drops. He is sure it did.

53

The green hose leads Frank to this big tree trunk.

"Who is back there? I think it's Jean. Is it? Is it Jean?" asks Frank.

"Yes, Frank. It's me. Did you get wet?" asks Jean. "I hope you think it was fun."

28A

The King's Song

by Clint Moscari

illustrated by Valerie Sokolova

In just a week, King Ming had his song back.

"Singing is my best thing," sang King Ming.

66

"Singing is my best thing," said King Ming. He sang to Queen Ling. He sang sweet tunes.

59

At five, Queen Ling sat. King Ming got set to sing his song, but no tune came out. King Ming did not sing his song.

"I will bring him sweet notes each time I come," said Green Bird.

"King Ming has lost his song. Can you teach King Ming to sing?" asked Queen Ling.

"I think I can teach him as quick as a wink," said Green Bird.

"Don't be sad, King Ming," said Queen Ling. "Maybe a bird can help you sing." Queen Ling wrote this note: Needed: Bird that can teach King Ming to sing.

64

61

31A

Red Bird came, but he had no songs. Pink Bird came, but he had no songs.

Then Green Bird came. He had sweet, sweet songs. His songs made King Ming and Queen Ling smile. Then Queen Ling spoke.

62

63

Call Kay if you
find this dog.
555-1234

"She is not a stray dog," Dad tells
Ray. "She has a tag. We will get
her food. Then we will call and tell
Kay to get her dog."

74

Ray Trains Dex

by Angie Tubbman

illustrated by Shirley Beckes

"Sit," Ray tells Dex. Dex sits.
"Good dog!"

67

33A

"Stay," Ray tells Dex.

At first Dex stays. He stays and waits when Ray tells him.

"This dog has a cut," Dad tells Ray. "It is not a bad cut."

Ray sees a rock on the ground. "I think she got cut on this rock. Do you think so, Dad?" asks Ray.

Dad nods as he checks the cut.

Dex sees a dog. The dog's tail is
going thump, thump. She is glad to
see Dex. Dex sniffs, sniffs, sniffs.

But then, Dex will not sit and
wait. He runs.

72

69

Dex runs fast. Ray and Dad run as fast as Dex.

"Stop, Dex," yells Ray. "Sit! Sit!" Dex sits and waits.

"I think I hear a dog whine," Dad tells Ray. "Maybe it needs help."

"Go," Ray tells Dex. Dex runs. So do Ray and Dad.

70

71

Sweet Treats
by Cyrus Rutherman

Kay has a huge tray filled with fresh green grapes. She can't wait, so she takes a big bunch!

"Yum! Yum! Yum!"

Grapes are a sweet treat. These kids like to snack on grapes every day. Would you like a bunch right now?

82

75

37A

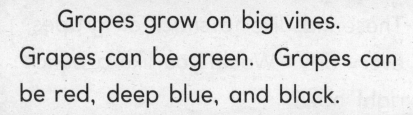

Grapes grow on big vines. Grapes can be green. Grapes can be red, deep blue, and black.

38A

See the sweet fresh grapes at this stand. Which fresh grapes would you snack on?

Trucks bring grapes to shops and stands. Fresh grapes cannot stay on trucks. Grapes may rot if they stay too long.

Lines and lines of grape plants grow in the ground. Grape plants need sun. Grape plants need rain.

80

77

39A

Grapes stay on vines a long time. After a wait, grapes will be ripe. Grapes take time to get big and plump and sweet.

78

Ripe grapes cannot stay on vines. Ripe grapes need to be picked when it is time. Ripe grapes must be picked by hand.

79

Well, sometimes beasts huff and puff. This beast huffs and puffs. This beast huffs and puffs and chases YOU!

90

What Will We Do?

by Mandy Jackson

illustrated by Nicole Wong

It's a hot, hot day. It is too hot to run and play. What can we do?

83

41A

We'd like to swim, but we can't. Bay Lake isn't open. What'll we do if we can't swim?

No, no, no! You must be mixed up. Beasts don't huff and puff. Beasts wail!

84

89

42A

Wait! That's not right! It
doesn't wail! It huffs and puffs!
Huff, huff, huff! Puff, puff, puff!

We can't play on the deck.
It has wet paint. What'll we do
if we can't play on the deck?

88

85

43A

We'll read! It'll be fun! Let's sit and read!

This tale is the best. A big, bad beast chases three nice pigs. It wails and wails. It trails those pigs home. It keeps on wailing and wailing!

86

87

44A

Nell, Ben, Fay, Blaine, and Jess
had a fine meal.

"Let's clean up," said Jess.

Under each plate was a thank
you note!

98

Let's Eat

by Robert Stewart

illustrated by John Segal

The day had ended. It was time to
eat. Nell had a plate filled with meat.

"It's time to get Ben," said Nell.
"He'd hate to be late."

91

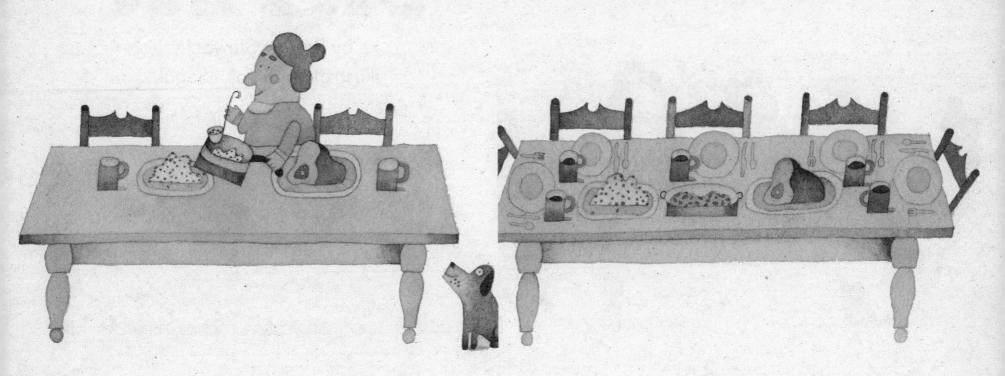

While Nell was out, Fay came in.
Fay had a pot filled with rice. She
put rice on a plate.

"Nell likes rice and peas. She'll
like this," said Fay.

Nell set five gray plates and five
red cups. Ben went and got Fay,
Blaine, and Jess.

92

97

Nell gave Ben a note.

Please come quick.

Let's have fun.

Your pals,

Nell and Ben

96

While Nell was out, Blaine came
in. Blaine had a pot filled with
beans. Blain put beans in a big dish.
"Ben likes beans. He'll like this,"
said Blaine.

93

Then Jess came in. Jess filled
each cup with grape drink.
"Nell likes grapes. She'll like this.
She will," said Jess.

Nell and Ben came home.
"Isn't this a treat?" asked Ben.
"Yes, it is," said Nell. "I didn't
make this, but I know who did."

94

95

48A

It Was Snow Fun

by Shira Alami

illustrated by Jamie Smith

"Did you have fun?" asked Mom.
"It was great when the wind didn't
blow. Then it was snow fun!" said Bill.
Joan just laughed.

106

Snow fell on the grass. Snow fell
on oak trees. Snow fell and fell.

99

49A

Bill was sleeping when it snowed.
When he woke up the snow was
there. Bill got up fast. Bill likes
snow. He likes snow a lot.

"Not in this wind. It is blowing
the snow. We must go in. Quick.
Let's go!" said Joan.

"Yes," said Bill. "Let's go!"

100

105

Bill made a little white snow cat.
Joan put a bow on it. It was cute.
"Can we make a snow dog,
Joan?" asked Bill when he was done.

104

Bill ran and woke up Joan. He
will show Joan the snow.
"Get up, Joan. Get up, get up!
It snowed, Joan!" said Bill.

101

51A

Joan got up.

"We can get dressed and put on hats and coats. Then we can go and play in the snow," said Joan.

Bill fell in the snow on his back. Joan fell in the snow, too. Bill made snow wings. Bill and Joan had snow all over them.

102

103

Boat Rides

by Redmond Turner

This boat is a huge ship. It can take long trips at sea. If you were on this ship, you could eat, sleep, and play games on it. Would that be great?

114

Is it time for a ride? A boat ride can be so much fun.

107

53A

This boat has sails as white as snow. The big white sails make the boat go. Wind blows and fills the sails.

This man rows with his left hand. Then he rows with his right hand. He will just keep rowing. Soon his boat will pick up speed.

This boat has no sail. It is not a raft. To make this boat go you must row. If you stop rowing, the boat will just float and drift off.

Strong winds can make the boat go fast! It is fun to sail, but you must stay safe. You need a life vest.

112

109

55A

This flat boat has no sails. It is slow. You use a pole to make it float. It can carry loads down this stream.

This boat is a raft. It is fun to ride fast on white waves. Hats and life vests help keep this ride safe.

Fun with Gram

by Frances Berry
illustrated by Judith Lanfredi

"We're playing dress up!" Joan and Rob laugh. "When we're at Gram's, we know we'll have fun!"

122

Joan can't wait to go to Gram's. She knows it will be fun. So far, they've cut rows of paper dolls. What's next?

115

Gram and Joan have a nice
snack. Then Gram has a plan.
"Let's go," she tells Joan. "I
know where we can have fun!"

116

Mom and Rob come in.
Gram tells Rob to see what
Pops left in the trunk. Rob sees
a big tan hat and a gray vest.

121

58A

Joan takes off the dress.
Then she sees a green silk hat.
She puts it on. It fits!

120

Gram shows Joan a huge, oak
trunk. It's loaded with things. Joan
sees coats and hats and a dress.

117

"Gram," she asks, "where did you get this green silk dress?"

"It's from Pops. Put it on."

Gram and Joan laugh.

118

Gram's green dress is so soft. The silk floats around Joan. Gram's face glows. Joan looks nice.

119

Rex Knows

by Paul Russell

illustrated by Susan Lexa

Rex is good at playing. He can
do tricks and make each friend smile.
Rex knows they're glad to see him.

130

"Wake up," Joan tells Rex. "It's
time for work."
Rex likes his job, so he gets up.

123

61A

Joan fills each bowl.

"Eat up so you can do a great job," Joan hints as Rex eats.

Joan and Rex get to work. Rex sits still while Joan rings the bell. Ring, ring, ring. Soon Rick lets Joan and Rex in.

124

129

62A

Joan stops and talks with Kate. "So, is it time for work, Rex?" asks Kate. "Must Rex go?"

"Yes, we're on our way," Joan tells Kate. "We'll have fun."

128

"Stay still," laughs Joan. "Slow down. We've no time to play. I must brush your coat so it feels soft."

125

63A

Then Joan gets her coat and the
leash. Rex and Joan go to work.
Joan knows that Rex likes his job so
much! Joan likes it, too.

126

On the way, Rex sees Nat and his
dog Duke. Nat knows that Rex can't
stop to play. Nat knows Rex must
get to his job on time.

127

Bedtime for Ray

by Tami Lo Verso

illustrated by Yvette Banek

Ray's dream is about his game.
In his dream, Ray wins the game.
What do you think Shep's
dream is?

It was bedtime. Ray didn't want
to go to bed yet. He wanted to play
his game. He wanted to win.

138

131

Ray is six. He can tell time. Ray's dad has a rule about bedtime. On a weekday, Ray's bedtime is at 8:00. It was that time.

132

Shep can't get on Ray's bed, but Shep has a rug. Shep sleeps on the rug at Ray's bedside.

137

At last, Ray gets in his bed. His mother reads him a nice bedtime tale. Shep is so big that he can't sleep on Ray's bed.

So Ray went up the steps. Shep went with him. Shep likes to be with Ray, and Ray likes to be with Shep.

136

133

Shep likes to watch Ray. Shep gets in the bathtub to see Ray brush his teeth. Ray can't let Shep do that. Shep can't be in the tub!

Ray must try to get Shep out. So Ray gets in the bathtub. Ray can't lift Shep up, but he gets Shep out. Shep grins as if it is a game.

134

135

68A

Then Pancake jumped on a
sailboat with big white sails. He
sailed and sailed and sailed.

146

Pancake Ran

retold by George O'Neal
illustrated by Carol Koeller

At sunrise, Midge and Madge got
up. Midge and Madge made a big,
big pancake.

139

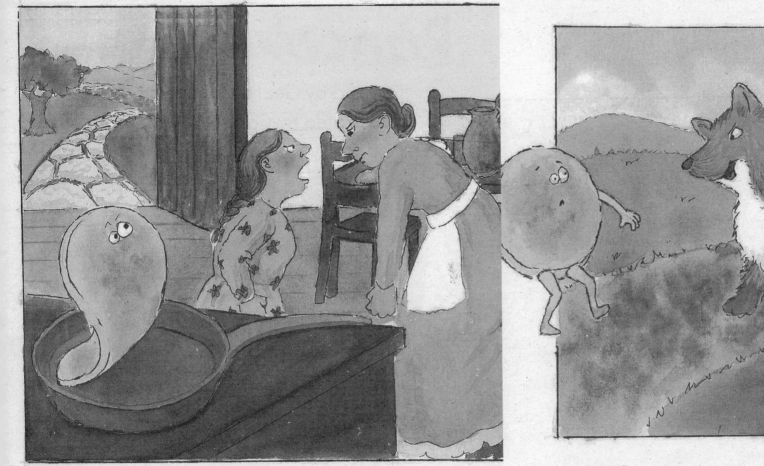

"This is just for me," said Midge.

"No, it is not," hissed Madge.

While Midge and Madge yelled,

Pancake jumped up.

"I am going on a trip," said
Pancake.

"I cannot hear you," said Fox.
"Get close."

But, Pancake just ran.

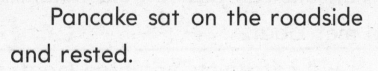

Pancake sat on the roadside
and rested.

"Where are you going?"
asked Fox.

Then Pancake ran out the door.
Midge and Madge ran after
Pancake. Midge and Madge did not
catch him.

144

141

Pancake ran down a hillside and met Sheep.

"I will catch you," boasted Sheep.

"Midge and Madge did not catch me," yelled Pancake as he ran. "You cannot catch me, Sheep."

142

Pancake ran past an old windmill and met Goat.

"I will catch you," grunted Goat.

"Midge, Madge, and Sheep did not catch me," yelled Pancake. "You can try, but you cannot catch me."

143

72A

A Springtime Rain

by Hilda Ramirez

We see a huge rainbow! The rainbow glows. Sunshine is on its way.

We like rain. We are glad when it rains. It's fun to be out in a springtime rain.

147

73A

Kay likes to walk her dog in the rain. Rain can wash pathways and make them clean.

148

Jane peeks out. She sees raindrops on the glass. Jane looks up.

"Quick!" Jane yells. "You must see this!"

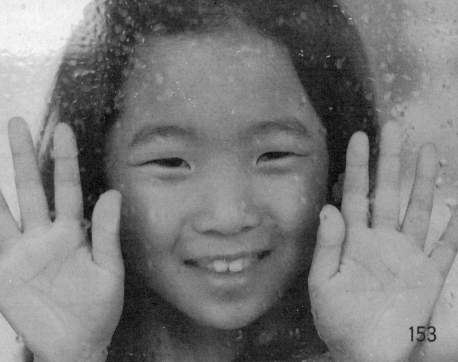

153

Kay sees raindrops shine on plants. Rain helps plants grow and spread.

When it rains a lot, we stay in. Swings and slides get wet, so we can't use them. We get a long playtime in class.

152

149

75A

Dad takes Quinn to class.
Quinn is dressed for rain. He has
his raincoat. He has a matching
rain hat on his head.

Beth and Gwen are dressed
for rain, too. Their mom watches
as they head to school. Gwen
holds Beth's hand.

76A

Rosebud

by Mary Martinez

illustrated by Benrei Huang

It was time to head to bed. It was bedtime on Rosebud.

162

My mother had a big white boat. Mom's big white boat was an old sailboat. Mom let me name it.

155

I chose "Rosebud." Mom got red
paint and paintbrushes. We painted
that name on the boat. I painted a
red rosebud.

The sun's rays spread. The sea
glowed yellow and red. Then no
more rays. The sun had set.

156

161

One time we went on a long trip.
We sailed and sailed. It was sunset,
but it was not bedtime yet.

160

Mom and I went sailing. We
sailed in the daytime. On nice days,
we set sail at sunrise. Sometimes we
sailed all day long.

157

79A

If it rained, we stayed inside the boat. We played games. We read. But sailing was more fun than being inside.

When the sun peeked out, we'd go up and sit topside. The sailboat rocked and we sang songs. We sang, "Row, row, row your boat."

158

159

Unit 5
Watch Us Grow

Contents

Mark Shark 1B

Clark's Part 5B

At the Shore 9B

More Fun for Jake 13B

See the Birds 17B

A Bath for Mert 21B

Fox and Crow 25B

Meet Gert 29B

Look at This! 33B

Two Good Cooks 37B

Good Homes 41B

Big Problems 45B

Moose's Tooth 49B

Moon News 53B

Boot's Clues 57B

Red Zed and Blue Stu 61B

Down on the Farm 65B

Scout and Count 69B

Dawn's Voice 73B

Shawn's Toys 77B

Mark Shark

by Melissa Rothman

illustrated by Teri Sloat

Mark and his pals play, and the dark sea is filled with sweet tunes.

10

Mark Shark saw this harp in the deep dark sea. Mark Shark had never seen a harp. Can he play it?

3

Mark plucked at the strings, and
sweet notes came out.

He played and played. Sweet
tunes filled the sea.

Mark was a huge star.

Mark's pals asked Mark to teach
them to play.

"It's not hard," said Mark.

4

9

2B

Carl just had to tell his pals. Carl and his pals swam back. His pals sang to the sweet tunes that Mark played.

Mark's pals had not seen him in a long time.

"I will swim and find Mark," said Carl. Will Carl find him?

8

5

3B

Carl can hear sweet tunes. He swam to see what made the sweet tunes. Then Carl saw Mark and his harp. Can Mark play it?

I didn't know you can play the harp," Carl told Mark.

"I just started and got better each day," said Mark.

6

7

Clark's Part

by Jay Griffin

illustrated by Adjoa Burrowes

That night, five kids marched on stage. Clark was not hard to see!

"I got a part in the class show," Clark told Mom. "I will be a big dog in the show."

18

11

"Five kids will put on dog masks and capes. We will march on stage and bark. Then we will say our parts," said Clark.

"Let's start to read your part," said Mom. "Let's start."

Mom is at the class show. Clark had on his mask and cape.

"Will you know me when I am on stage?" asked Clark.

"I will know your bark," said Mom, with a smile.

12

17

6B

His classmates wrote on his cast.
"Can you write?" asked Rick.

"Maybe with my left hand," said Clark.

"I hope you can still play your part," said Nell.

While Clark rode his bike that weekend, he said his part. A cat darted in his way. Clark turned his bike. Clark missed that cat, but he fell hard on the park path.

16

13

7B

Clark had sharp pain in his arm.
He needed a cast on his arm.

Clark had to start to do things
with his left hand.

14

15

8B

Carl hopes he can get a sailboat. Carl will sail far. Then he will head back home at the shore.

At the Shore

by Jared Chiang

This is the shore. It is where land and sea meet.

26

19

Carl and Tess see seagulls. More and more seagulls will come. Seagulls hunt for food in the sea and on the shore.

You can see sand, grass, and shells on the shore.

Unit 5/Lesson 21/Selection 3

10B

Carl sees a crab in its shell. The crab will grow too big for that shell. Then it must find a shell that fits!

Carl's home is on the shore. Carl can see the sea from his window.

24

21

Mom, Carl, and Jill go for a short walk. Jill likes to see waves crash on the shore.

Tess is Carl's pal. She hunts for pretty seashells.

More Fun for Jake

by Melissa Rothman

illustrated by John Hovell

The race was more fun than Jake thought it would be.

"Let's race!" yelled Jake.

"Yes we will, but let's wait for the weekend," said Dad.

34

Every day Jake's dad runs on the shore. Dad runs and runs.

27

13B

"When I grow up, I will run like my dad. I will be fast, and I will run far," thought Jake. "I will be fast like him."

On the day of the race, Jake wore his green shorts and his red cap. Mom came to clap for Jake and Dad.

28

33

14B

"Would you like to be in that race?" Dad asked Jake.

"Yes, yes, yes!" said Jake. "I can be in it."

32

One day Jake and his dad went to a sports store.

"I like these green shorts and this red cap," Jake told his dad.

29

When the weekend came, Dad asked Jake to run with him. Jake wore his green shorts and red cap. Dad and Jake ran and ran.

Each weekend Jake and Dad ran. One day, Jake showed Dad a note. It said, "Race for Dads and Cubs." Can Dad and Jake race?

30

31

See the Birds

by Susie Dietz

This is not a chick. It is a young bird with dark spots. When she is grown up, she will look just like her mom. She will make her own nest and have her own baby birds.

42

Look at this bird perched on a tree branch. She has a sweet song. Chirp, chirp, chirp. She can chirp a pretty song.

35

It is fall. The bird that is perched in this tree will find lots to eat. Every time he turns, he will see a treat.

Four baby birds sit in this nest. They perk up when mom bird brings food.

36

41

The first baby bird will burst its shell. The chick cannot see yet, but it can peep.

When it turns cold, it is hard to get food. This bird gets food in wet snow.

40

37

19B

It is spring. This bird has made her nest with sticks, wet dirt, and soft grass. She sits in her nest.

Her eggs will be safe in this nest. The chicks are curled up inside the eggs. They will not be hurt.

38

39

A Bath for Mert

by Maryann Cristensen

illustrated by Lizi Boyd

"Mom, we gave Mert the best bath," Burt boasted.

Mert barked and barked.

"Maybe Mert gave you baths, too!" said Mom.

"Where is Mert?" asked Kate.

Mert was curled up under the porch.

"She is sleeping in the soft dirt," said Burt.

50

43

Mert woke up and jumped to greet Kate.

Kate turned and said, "Mert has dirt on her fur. Mert needs a bath."

Then Mert started to shake, shake, and shake.

"Stop, Mert," yelled Kate. "Don't shake so much. My shirt and skirt are soaked!"

44

49

22B

Kate grasped the hose to spray
Mert, but Kate sprayed Burt.
"Stop!" yelled Burt. "You're
squirting me. My shirt is soaked."

"Yes," said Burt. "Just follow me.
First, we fill this tub with water. Then
we stir in soap flakes."

48

45

23B

Kate and Burt plunked Mert in
the tub. Kate and Burt had to scrub
hard until Mert was clean.

"Hold Mert for me," said Kate.
"Get a firm grip on her, so I can
squirt and take off the suds."

46

47

Fox and Crow

retold by Melissa Rothman
illustrated by Tom Sperling

Fox tricked Crow this time, but Crow has learned. Fox will not trick her next time!

58

Crow is perched in a birch tree. She sees some grapes on the ground.

51

Crow grabs the grapes and goes
back to her perch.

The grapes land in soft dirt.
As Crow sings, Fox eats them up.
Then he smiles, turns, and trots off.

52

57

Then Fox tells Crow, "It's sad that a bird as nice as you cannot sing."

Crow whirls, and then she blurts, "Sir, I am learning to sing!"

Fox passes by. It seems as if he has not had a meal in years.

Fox thinks, "If that bird speaks, she will drop those grapes."

56

53

27B

First Fox asks, "What is your name?"
Crow turns her back.

Next Fox asks, "Crow, are you feeling well?"
Crow will not speak. Crow will not stir.

54

55

28B

Meet Gert

by Carmen Santos

illustrated by John Kurtz

This is Gert with me. We met in first grade. Now it is Gert's turn to write about me!

This is my friend Gert. She is eight years old. She is in third grade. I wrote about Gert. Turn the pages and meet Gert.

66

59

This is Gert at the beach with
her mom. She begins her day in the
shade. She doesn't want to burn.
She is reading about surfing.

This is Gert in a pink skirt.
She has burst on to the stage and
is whirling and whirling. Gert has
fun whirling.

60

65

30B

This is Gert at a race. She has on a white shirt and shorts. Gert is crossing the red line first. She will win first prize.

This is Gert with her pictures of birds chirping. Gert likes to take pictures of birds perched in trees. Gert likes red birds. She likes red the best.

64

61

31B

This is Gert on a team. She plays sports with girls her age. Gert is good at kicking. She and her teammates have on red shirts and shorts.

This is Gert on skates. She has on a green shirt and skirt. Gert is just learning to turn on one leg. Gert likes when her skirt spins.

62

63

Look at This!

by Louise Tidd

illustrated by Marilyn Janovitz

"Look at these plants! What can we do with them?" asked Tad.

"We can eat them," said Mom.

"Such good prizes!" said Tad.

"Mom," said Tad, "let's go for a nice bike ride along the path."

Tad and Mom got on this big bike. They took a ride on a bike path.

74

When Mom and Tad got back
again, Tad saw Trish.

"Let's go and see Trish," said Tad.
"Trish is in her yard."

Tad and Mom had to water their
plants and pull up weeds. Tad and
Mom saw their plants grow big.

"Look," yelled Tad. "Look at these
big plants."

68

73

34B

Tad and Mom took the seeds
and went home. Tad made holes in
the dirt. Then he put seeds in them.
Mom put dirt over the seeds that
Tad planted.

"What is this?" asked Mom.
"I am planting seeds. Green
bean plants and green pea plants will
grow," said Trish. Then Trish stood up.

72

69

35B

"Can we plant seeds, Mom?"
asked Tad. "It looks like fun."

"We can, but it is not just fun,"
said Mom. "It is work."

70

Trish gave them some seeds.

"Growing these plants is fun and
work. If you work hard you will get a
good prize," said Trish.

71

36B

Mom laughs and sits.
"This is a real treat. You and
Dad did a good deed!" said Mom.

82

Two Good Cooks

by Gretchen Nguyen
illustrated by Laura Rader

Mom is on her way home. Mom
will be late. My father and I will
cook. We began with a good plan.

75

We look at this shelf. We see
eggs and ham and cheese and milk.
Those will be good to cook with.

Just then I see Mom.

"That smells so good! What is
it?" she asks. "Can I look?"

"Just sit and we will bring it to
you," I say. "Then you can look."

76

81

38B

I mix eggs and milk. Dad cuts
ham and cheese into bits. Then I mix
ham and cheese in with the eggs.
Dad will heat the eggs, ham, and
cheese in a pan.

We take out eggs, ham, cheese,
and milk. Then we get bowls and
forks and pans. We can't cook yet.

80

77

Dad hands me Mom's cookbook.
It will tell us how to cook. We look
at the page that shows us how to
cook eggs. This is it!

This cookbook tells us to get eggs,
milk, ham, and cheese.

"This looks good!" I say. "We
have eggs, milk, ham, and cheese."

78

79

Good Homes

by Louise Tidd

Hives, caves, and burrows make good animal homes. This is not an animal home. It is for kids. Can you tell what it is?

These insects are bees.
Can you hear them buzz?

90

83

41B

Bees live together in hives.
Hives are good homes for bees.

If one rabbit sees a problem, it
thumps its foot. Then the rabbits
run back in their burrow to be safe.

42B

This cute fellow is a rabbit. Rabbits dig burrows. A burrow is a big hole.

Each hive has a queen. The queen bee does nothing but lay eggs. That is her job. These bees feed their queen bee.

43B

Caves make good homes for bats. Bats sleep all day. They hook their back feet in cracks. Bats sleep upside down.

It is dark when bats wake up. Bats hear much better than they can see. Bats make squeaks to tell if it is safe.

Big Problems

by Jackson Prescott

illustrated by Shari Halpern

Dennis and Ray can fit in the big house. Dennis likes that. Ray likes it, too. Dennis and Ray like to be together.

"No problems," said Ray.

Ray is a boy. He has a dog. Ray's dog is Dennis. Dennis had problems that began when he was just a pup.

98

91

45B

Dennis was much too big to fit in his dog bed. It was a problem.

"Dennis needs a big bed," said Ray. "Yes, Dennis needs a big bed."

"We can make a big house for Dennis," said Dad.

So Ray, his sister, and his dad made a big house for Dennis.

92

97

As Dennis got big, so did his problems. When Dennis stood up, he did not fit in his dog house.

"You need a big house," said Ray.

96

Ray gave Dennis big soft yellow pillows. Did Dennis like his yellow bed? Dennis did. It was nice and soft. Better yet, it was big.

93

As Dennis got big, his problems got big as well. It was hard for Ray to take Dennis for a walk.

"This is a problem," said Ray. "It is a big problem."

So, Ray began to ride on, not walk with, Dennis. Did Dennis like this? Dennis did. Did Ray like this? Ray did like it. Dad did, too.

"No problem," said Ray.

94

95

48B

Moose's Tooth

by Paul Giuliano

illustrated by Sachiko Yoshikawa

Moose likes his new brew.
Moose's loose tooth likes it, too.

Moose has a loose tooth. His loose tooth feels funny. A loose tooth can go back and forth.

106

99

49B

Moose likes to eat water plants.
Moose has to get in deep water up
to his knees.

Moose adds milk. His green goop
shake is ready. Moose can drink it.
Moose has no need to chew!

100

105

50B

Moose adds plants and a flower or two to the mix. His plant and flower mix looks like thick green goop.

Moose dips down and scoops up a plant. Moose's food is wet. Dip and scoop! Dip and scoop!

104

101

Moose has a loose tooth. Now, Moose can't chew his food. Chewing can make his tooth too loose. Moose must get a new plan.

Moose has a new plan. Moose takes his food inside. He knows just what to do. If Moose can't chew, he will mix a brew. That is his plan.

102

103

Moon News

by James Franklin

Moon Song

I like to look at the moon,
and hope to visit it soon.
You can come, too.
You can be in my crew.

This is our moon. We can see the moon at night. We cannot see it at noon. That's a scoop! No moon at noon.

114

107

This is a full moon. It can look
white. It can look yellow. It can look
sort of red. A full moon is pretty,
white, yellow, or red.

This painting also shows the
moon. This painting shows what the
moon shone on. It shone on water.
Water gleams in the moon's glow.

108

113

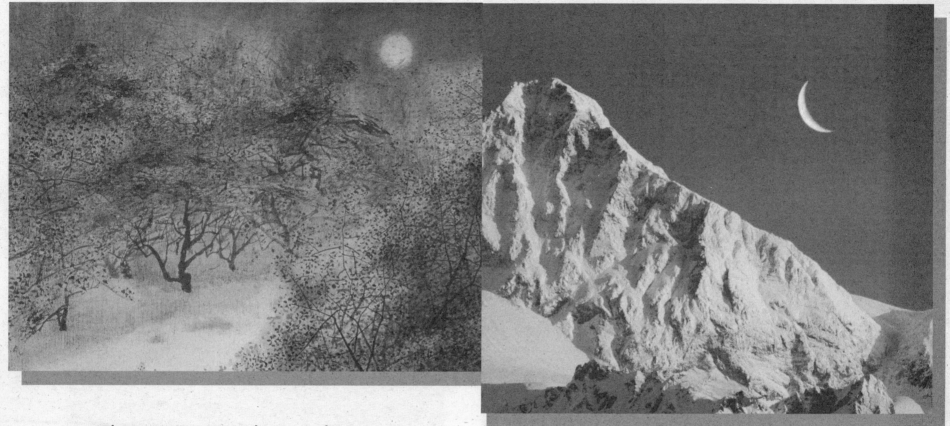

This painting shows the moon. This painting also shows what the moon shone on. It shone on land. It shone on trees. Trees gleam in the moon's glow.

This is a new moon. It looks like a slice of moon. But it is not a moon slice. A new moon shows just the part that is lit up.

112

This moon chart shows you how the moon can look. This moon chart starts with the new moon on day 1. It shows the full moon on day 14.

Look at this painting. It shows the moon and stars. Did the person who painted this like the moon? Did he add anything to it?

110

111

Boot's Clues

by Cindy Detmar
illustrated by
Bill Brandon

"You did it, Boot!" said Sue. "You are cute! You give clues and you get clues."

Here is a tale about Boot and Sue. I hope you like it! This tale is just for you.

122

115

Drew had to take a trip. He left
Boot with Sue.

"Thanks," Drew said. "Boot's clues
will tell you what to do."

Then Sue gave a clue. She turned
off the light to see if Boot would hop
upon his bed. Did he do it?

116

121

58B

"That is a neat clue, Boot!" said
Sue. "You let me know that you need
food and water."

Boot ran and ran. He picked up
a stick and gave it to Sue.

"Is this a clue?" asked Sue.

"What kind of clue is this, Boot?"
Boot gave Sue a grin.

120

117

Sue threw the stick. Boot
jumped up.

"He got it! It's a clue!"
yelled Sue.

Sue and Boot went inside.
Boot bumped his food bowl
with his nose.

"Is this a clue?" asked Sue.

Red Zed and Blue Stu

by Kate Pistone

illustrated by Paulette Bogan

Now, Red Zed and Blue Stu were warm and full. They did not say a thing. They just ate grass.

Red Zed is a mule. Blue Stu is a mule. Red Zed and Blue Stu live on the same hill. The hill has grass for them to eat.

130

123

61B

One day, cool winds blew.

"Blue Stu, it is too cool on this hill," said Red Zed.

Blue Stu did not say a thing. He just ate grass.

Red Zed saw no grass.

"I need food, too," said Red Zed. "I need food to eat."

"Let's go back to our cool hill," said Blue Stu. He had a plan.

124

129

"It is warm on this dune," said
Red Zed.

"Yes, but I need food," said Blue
Stu. "Let's look for grass."

"Yes, yes," said Red Zed. "Let's!"

128

"Let's look for a new home. I like
warm places," Red Zed went on.

"Let me chew this last bit of
grass. I will be ready at noon," said
Blue Stu. "I need a few more chews."

125

63B

Blue Stu and Red Zed left the hill.
They got in this crude boat.
Blue Stu rowed and rowed.

"Land ho!" yelled Red Zed. "Land
ho! Land ho!"

"I hope there is grass," grunted
Blue Stu.

126

127

64B

Down on the Farm
by Siri Hansen

This hen is with her baby chicks.
Her family stays with her for now.

It's spring down on the farm. It
is time to shout, "Come and see each
animal and its family!"

138

It is spring on this farm. Come
and see a farm animal here.

131

Up on a hill is a brown horse with white feet. Her foal is with her. Her foal is growing up now.

132

The wool coat on this mother sheep is thick and soft! She is with her lamb. Soon her lamb will have a thick, soft coat, too.

137

Look at this proud mother pig and her family. She sniffs the ground with her snout. Soon her seven piglets will be as big as their mom.

136

Out in the grass is a brown and white cow with her brown and white baby. Her baby is growing up now.

133

This cute wood mouse skips along the ground. This mouse likes to sneak into the barn. It likes to get bits of food in the barn.

A barn owl sits in this barn. If the mouse sees the barn owl, the mouse will not go in. Barn owls help keep mice out of barns.

Scout and Count

by Tawana Ross

illustrated by Philomena O'Neill

"Wow! Count knows his name now!" shouted Scout. "Bow wow," barked Count.

146

Scout sat on the couch when Dad came into the house. In his arms was a sweet brown and white pup.

139

"Miss Crown gave us this pup.
Will we keep him, Scout?"

"Wow!" said Scout. "Yes! Please,
let's keep him. He's so cute. He's a
sweet pup."

One day, Scout played out in the
yard. Count sat with Dad. Count
and Dad sat on the deck.

"Here, Count," shouted Scout.
Count jumped down off the deck and
ran to Scout.

140

145

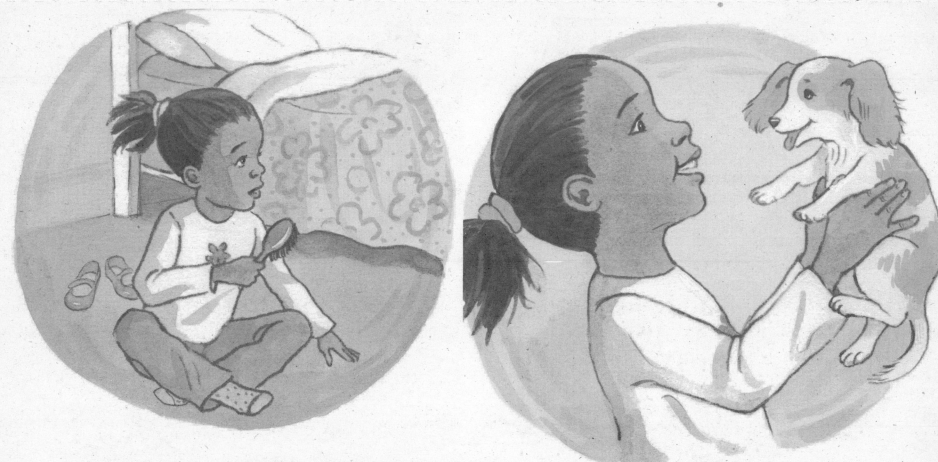

Scout found a brush for Count's coat. Scout did not see Count.

"Here, Count," shouted Scout.

Count did not come to her. So Scout found Count, sat down, and brushed his coat.

"What will we name him?" asked Dad. "How about Sprout?"

Scout frowned. Then she asked, "Can we name him Count?"

"Count is a good name," said Dad.

144

141

"Here, Count," Scout shouted as Count sniffed around his new house. Count did not come.

"I will teach Count myself," vowed Scout. "It will be like dog school!"

Scout found a bowl for food. "Here, Count," shouted Scout. Count did not come. So Scout took that bowl to Count and fed him. Count ate and ate.

142

143

Dawn's Voice

by Eileen Brady

illustrated by Tim Bowers

With joy, Dawn joined the school party. Paul thanked Dawn.

"My loud voice was just right!" Dawn shouted. Then she said with her soft voice, "Just right."

154

Dawn had a nice voice. Outside, her voice was loud. Inside, her voice was soft.

147

73B

At times, Dawn forgot which
voice to use. If she forgot at home,
Mom would say, "Use an inside
voice, Dawn."

148

Paul did hear it. He looked up
and made the catch. Dawn's team
got the win.

153

Dawn shouted to Paul, "Look up, Paul! Look up!"

Dawn's loud voice filled the park. Would Paul hear it?

If she forgot at school, Miss Law would whisper, "Too much noise. How can we read? Use an inside voice, Dawn."

152

149

Last week, Dawn was at a school game. Her school's Red Team led the game. The Yellow Team was at bat. The batter swung and hit hard.

150

151

Shawn's Toys

by Eileen Brady

illustrated by Steven Parton

"This toy is the best for me," said Shawn. "It is the best!"

"Good choice," said Dad. "Good choice, Shawn. We will get that."

162

Each day Shawn put coins in his big plastic jar. Shawn would be glad when his coins filled the jar. Soon Shawn could buy a new toy.

155

At night, Shawn dreamed about toys. In his dreams, he saw rows and rows of toys. He had dream toys.

156

Shawn saw a brown stuffed toy with black paws. He pointed at it. "Please," shouted Shawn. "This is it! I will buy this toy."

161

Then Roy pointed at a toy boat.
"This boat can be launched in a
pond," said Roy. "It's so much fun.
You will like this toy."

160

One day, Shawn put five coins in
his jar. "It's full," yelled Shawn.
No more coins would fit.

157

79B

Shawn dumped his coins. Dad joined Shawn as he counted his coins.

"Let's go to City Toys now. Do you know just what you will get?" asked Dad.

"No, but I will know it when I see it," said Shawn.

158

Dad and Shawn entered City Toys. Shawn saw rows of toys, just like in his dreams.

Roy showed them toys. He pointed to toy trains that could haul loads.

Shawn saw trains, trains, trains.

159

Unit 6

Three Cheers for Us!

Contents

Bears 1C

Hiding and Seeking 5C

Henry and Dad Go Camping 9C

Speedy and Chase 13C

The Three Races 17C

Seed Sisters 21C

The Fox and the Grapes 25C

Jingle, Jangle, and Jiggle 29C

Sally Jane and Beth Ann 33C

Ty and Big Gilly 37C

Bird Watching 41C

Benches 45C

Quiz Game 49C

Jack and the Beans 53C

Ruth's Day 57C

Stew for Peg 61C

Amy Ant 65C

Julie and Jason 69C

Home at Last 73C

Soccer 77C

Bears

by Anne Miranda

This bear likes sleeping at night with the moon shining above. It stretched and nodded off. Sleep well, bear! Sleep well!

10

What things do bears like? Just look and see!

3

Bears like eating. This black bear is sitting up in a tree. It is getting nuts. It grabbed them and ate them. It likes eating nuts!

This bear likes digging. It has been digging a den. It will line its den with branches and grass. Grass makes a soft mattress. It will be a nice bed to nap in.

4

9

This bear likes napping. It can sleep well even during the day. It will wake up and go trotting off to look for food. It will eat and nap again. This bear likes napping a lot.

Bears like fishing. Fishing is best when streams are filled with fish. Fast swimming fish race past this bear. They are racing up stream.

8

5

3C

Bears like swimming. It is a thrill to see this big, white bear swimming in the sea! It is bobbing up and down in the waves like floating ice. It swims toward the ice.

This bear has an itch. He likes scratching. He is rubbing his back on that tree. He looks as if he is grinning. He must have found just the spot to scratch.

6

7

4C

Hiding and Seeking

by Lance Langley

illustrated by Dominic Catalano

Miss Fox spotted Jill at last! Miss Fox tagged her. Jill was out. Jill was good at hiding, but Miss Fox was great at seeking!

18

The kits liked their first grade teacher, Miss Fox. Miss Fox liked them, and she liked playing games. She was fun!

11

5C

At playtime, the kits begged for a game of Hide and Seek. Miss Fox was IT. Miss Fox counted to ten. Her class hid while she counted.

Miss Fox hunted up and down for Jill. Jill had fun fooling Miss Fox. Jill's laughs made Jill's tree shake. Miss Fox saw it shaking.

12

17

6C

Jill was hiding in a good place. She hid in a tree above Miss Fox. Miss Fox looked and looked but she didn't see Jill. Jill smiled.

16

Red was hiding in a good place, but he did not sit still. He wagged his tail. Miss Fox spotted Red. She tagged him. Red was out.

13

7C

Meg was hiding in this very good place, but her ears jutted out. Miss Fox spotted Meg. She tagged her. Meg was out.

Blaze was hiding in a good place, but he clapped and hummed. Miss Fox spotted Blaze. She tagged him. Blaze was out.

14

15

Henry and Dad Go Camping

by Ting Biderman

illustrated by Stacey Schuett

Henry felt silly but safe. He felt sleepy, too. He went to sleep as his flat bed hissed its last hiss.

26

Dad put up the tent. Henry hurried to pump up the beds. Dad was sleepy, but Henry gazed up at the stars.

19

Then Henry sat up surprised.
What was that hissing sound? Henry
poked his dad and woke him up.

Dad flashed the light inside
the tent.

"Look at your bed, Henry,"
said Dad. "It's getting as flat
as a pancake. Your leaky bed
is hissing, not snakes."

"What's hissing?" Dad asked.

"It's creepy," said Henry. "It must be snakes!"

"Snakes?" asked Dad. "Maybe."

"No," Dad said. "It's not hissing. It's just a rope."

"The hissing hasn't stopped! What can it be?" Henry asked.

24

21

Dad shined a light toward
the grass.

"I can see something that's long
and thin like a snake," Dad said.
"Is it hissing?" asked Henry.

22

23

Speedy had planned on winning,
but Chase was first. Chase was the
winner!

34

Speedy and Chase

by Christopher K. Lyne

illustrated by Rick Stromoski

It was sunny but not too hot. It
was a good day for a race. Goats,
pigs, and cows lined up in the field.
They would get a good look.

27

Chase looked at Speedy. Chase studied him. Speedy hopped in place. Chase hoped he could keep up with Speedy. Was Speedy as speedy as he looked?

Chase pushed on toward the finish line. Chase didn't give up. He kept on going. Fans clapped and yelled. Speedy woke up surprised!

28

33

14C

"I plan on winning this race!" shouted Speedy.

"You seem fast," said Chase.

"Yes!" Speedy grinned. "Fast and planning on winning. It will be easy!"

Speedy was still napping when Chase jogged by. He was running at his own slow pace. He was smiling, too.

32

29

"Get ready. Go!" yelled Sheep.
Speedy zoomed past clapping
fans. Speedy really was speedy!
Chase jogged past them at his own
slow pace.

Speedy took the lead. "Chase
can't catch up," Speedy bragged. "I
feel a bit sleepy. I will win even if I
take a nap!"
He flopped down and napped.

30

31

16C

The cars raced at the same speed.
Fran's car was not faster. Ken's car
was not faster. That made Fran and
Ken happy, too!

42

The Three Races

by Madeleine Jeffries
illustrated by Amanda Harvey

Fran had her box of cars. She
and Ken each chose two racecars.

35

Ken picked a slick red racecar.
Fran picked next. She chose a much
bigger blue car. Fran hoped it was
faster, too. Speedier cars win!

Ken and Fran had one last race.
Fran's speedy blue car raced Ken's
fast striped car.
Which car would be faster?

36

41

18C

In the next race, Ken's striped car raced Fran's green car. This time, Ken's car zoomed faster. It was fast enough to win. It made Ken happy.

40

Then Ken picked a racecar with black stripes. Fran picked next. Fran picked a green car. It was nicer and had fatter wheels than Ken's.

37

In the first race, Fran's bigger blue car raced Ken's slick red car. Ken and Fran lined them up at the top of the hill.

Fran's car zipped faster than Ken's. Ken's car was much slower. Fran's car raced fast enough to win. That made Fran happy.

38

39

20C

Seed Sisters

by Anne Miranda

illustrated by Janet Pedersen

The plants are in bloom. How nice the backyard looks! Rose and Liz think their yard is the nicest yard in town!

It is spring. Liz and Rose are shopping for seeds. Liz and Rose always plant seeds in the spring.

50

43

21C

Rose picks a smaller pack of
seeds. Liz's pack is much bigger.
Liz and Rose go back home to plant
the seeds that they just got.

44

Liz's plants grow higher than
Rose's plants. Rose's are shorter.
Rose and Liz tell stories as they
wait for the plant buds to open!

49

22C

All spring the plants grow. They grow bigger and bigger and bigger each day. Liz's plants are different from Rose's.

Liz and Rose see that the seeds in each pack are different. Rose's seeds are much smaller and rounder. Liz's seeds are much longer and flatter.

48

45

Liz and Rose dig. Liz digs faster than Rose. Liz plants her seeds first. Rose digs slower than Liz. Rose plants her seeds last.

The seeds sprout. Liz's seeds sprout quicker. Rose's seeds are slower to sprout. Liz and Rose rake and weed their backyard plot once.

46

47

Digger puts the benches back in place. Gram will ask Digger back when the grapes get ripe. Digger can't wait! Those grapes are much tastier when they are ripe!

58

25C

The Fox and the Grapes

retold by Lindsey Pare
illustrated by Jeff Mack

Digger Fox is always happy to see Gram. Gram has a big back porch. Digger is happiest there. Grapes grow near that porch.

51

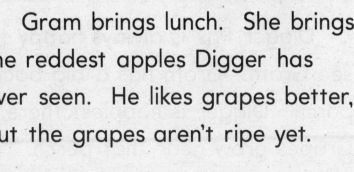

"Yuck," he grumbles. "It tastes like a pickle!"

"Yes," winks Gram. "The grapes aren't ripe yet. Next time, trust me."

Gram brings lunch. She brings the reddest apples Digger has ever seen. He likes grapes better, but the grapes aren't ripe yet.

52

57

Gram goes inside. Digger has a plan. He jiggles the benches closer to the grapes. He just has to have a grape!

Gram reaches for a grape and hands it to Digger. He tastes it.

56

53

27C

Gram cuddles Digger and tells him, "You must be the luckiest little fox ever. I got here just in time."

"Can't I eat one grape, Gram?" asks Digger.

Digger jiggles himself up. He reaches for the biggest bunch of grapes. He wiggles up, up, up. Then Digger tumbles down. Gram catches him.

54

28C

55

Jingle, Jangle, and Jiggle

by Jose Pitkin

illustrated by Judy Stead

Jiggle puts on his nose. He gives it the biggest, loudest, silliest honk he can! Then Jingle, Jangle, and Jiggle take a bow.

66

Jingle, Jangle, and Jiggle are pals. Jingle is the shortest. Jiggle is the biggest. Jangle is in the middle.

59

Jingle, Jangle, and Jiggle are clowns. Clowns make us chuckle and giggle. They always dress in funny hats and pants. They put on funny noses.

60

Jiggle jumps up. The bird zooms high. Jiggle cannot catch it. Then the bird dips low. Jiggle tackles that bird. He snatches his nose back!

65

30C

Jiggle sobs and sniffles. "I need my nose," he mumbles. Then a blue bird comes near. Jiggle's nose dangles from the bird's beak!

64

Jiggle has the longest nose. It makes a loud honking sound. Now it is missing! Where can it be? It is a puzzle. Jiggle must get it back!

61

Jiggle looks inside Jangle's boots. He looks inside Jingle's hat. Jiggle does not see his nose. He starts to grumble.

Jiggle looks in high places. Jingle looks in low places. Silly Jangle looks in a popcorn box! Jiggle's nose is still missing.

Sally Jane and Beth Ann

by James McKinley

illustrated by Tom Leonard

Sally Jane flew high across the sky. Beth Ann was in her grasp. They landed in the cave. Beth Ann thanked Sally Jane. Sally Jane was happy to help her new buddy, Beth Ann.

Sally Jane was a large brown bat. She spent much of her time hanging by her feet in her safe, dark cave.

74

67

33C

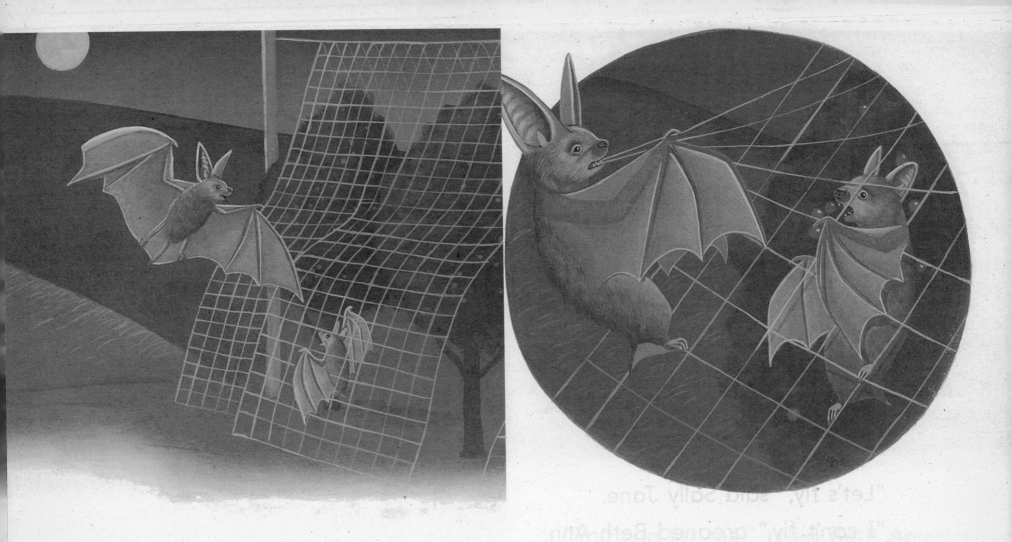

"My wing is snagged in this net,"
Beth Ann cried.

"I will try to get you out," Sally
Jane said with a bright smile.

Sally Jane gave it her best try.
She tugged and bit at the net. At
last, Beth Ann got free!

70

71

36C

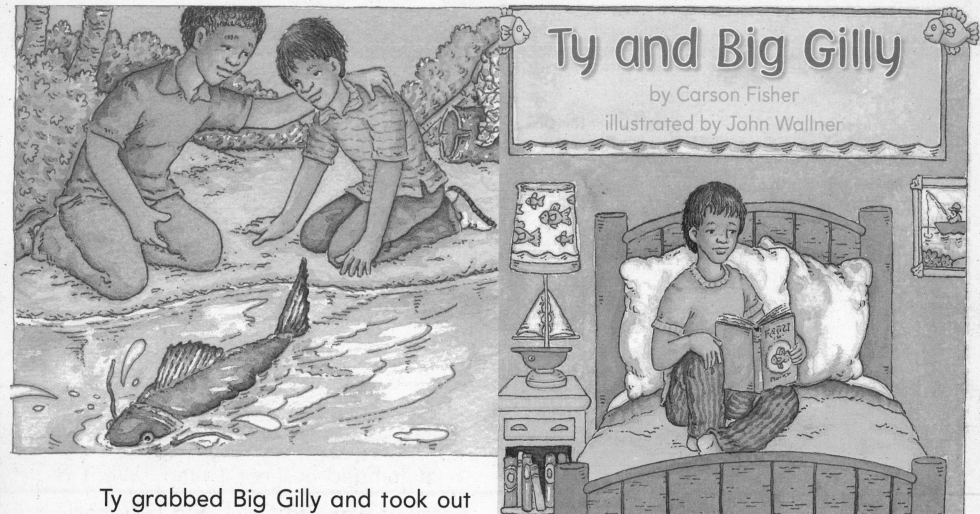

Ty and Big Gilly

by Carson Fisher

illustrated by John Wallner

Ty grabbed Big Gilly and took out the hook. He let Big Gilly go. Big Gilly swam off, still king of Sand Lake. Dad winked at Ty. He was glad Ty let Big Gilly go.

82

Ty had a hobby that made him happy. His hobby was fishing. Ty liked fishing.

75

Ty had a large fishing box. He kept it right by his bed. It was filled with hooks, jelly bugs, and all sorts of fishing stuff. It also had a fly that his dad had made.

It jumped a second time. What a sight! It was Big Gilly! Big Gilly had a big head. Its tail snapped back and forth. "That's the biggest fish in Sand Lake," Dad cried out.

76

81

38C

Then Ty had a bite! Ty had to reel it in. He gave it his best try. The fish was fighting hard. Then the fish on his line jumped up and out of the water. It was big!

One bright, sunny day, Ty and his dad went fishing. Ty had his fishing box, rod, and reel. He and Dad hiked to Sand Lake.

80

77

Ty sat under the pale blue sky as he baited his hook. He used a jelly bug. Ty closed his fishing box lid. Ty tried to keep the box neat and clean.

Ty threw back his line. He let it fly high across the lake. His jelly bug landed with a plop! Dad cast his line. Ty and Dad waited.

Bird Watching

by Rebecca McDermott

What can this bird do best?
It sings the sweetest songs.
Hush.   You might hear it!

This is a large bird. Three
large eggs can fit in its nest.
That huge nest is quite a sight!

This hawk can take flight high across the sky. Then it can dive down in a flash. It can fly faster than a racecar can race!

Which bird is the fastest swimmer? Few birds swim, but this one can zoom right by. It looks like it is flying in water!

44C

Benches

by Jillian Raymundo

illustrated by Elizabeth Sayles

Benches for you and benches for me,
on city streets or at the sea!
I should sit and you should, too,
on benches at parks or at the zoo!

Benches! Benches! Benches! See
them in cities. See them in towns.
See them in parks. See them at
beaches. Benches! Benches!

98

91

45C

Benches are like outside couches.
They are good places to sit. Kids
sit on benches in yards and parks.
Buddies can sit side by side and chat.

Moms, dads, and kids sit on
benches at beaches. This dad likes
to watch the sea flow in and out.
What a sight!

92

97

46C

Kids play games on benches. Some kids are winners. Some kids don't win. Still, kids like playing games outside.

Dogs and puppies go out on leashes. Grown-ups, kids, and pets sit on benches. Benches are good for sitting and resting.

96

93

Kids eat lunch on benches.
Many kids have lunchboxes. When
lunchtime is over the kids might sit
and rest on benches. Then they
might play ball or jump rope.

Kids read books on benches. Kids
read the funnies and comics, too. Kids
read on benches when it is sunny and
bright. When it rains, benches are not
good places for reading.

94

95

Quiz Game

by Cindy Wahl

Did you like this quick quiz? Was it fun? Do you have any ideas for a new quiz?

Hello! This book has a quick quiz on each page. I'm hopeful that you'll like this book. I like it a lot.

106

99

Which animal can sing sweetly?
Which can purr softly? Which can
growl loudly? Which can make
a squeaky sound?

Which bird can fly? Which can
swim in icy water? Which has bright
feathers? Which has long legs?

100

105

50C

Which animal has a shell? Which animals are furry? Which is a dog? Which is a cat? Which is the biggest?

Which animal can zip by quickly? Which will go by slowly? Which can wiggle by in a zigzag path? Which can go by in a leap?

104

101

51C

Which animal has long, helpful claws? Which has a big hump? Which can be stinky? Which looks spotty?

102

Which fish looks like a snake? Which has three white stripes? Which has five black stripes? Which has more than six legs?

103

52C

Jack and the Beans

by Anthony Swede

illustrated by Holli Conger

Jack and Jill picked bagful after bagful of beans. Those beans would last them a long, long time. Jack and Jill were thankful that Jack had such a good idea.

Jack and Jill had a big plot of land and a nice fat cow, but Jack and Jill did not have much food. Jack and Jill ate their last handful of oatmeal.

114

107

Jack had an idea. He took his nice fat cow to town. He could sell his cow and get food.

Jack was gone a long, long time. Jill did not feel happy.

Soon, the beans sprouted. Jack and Jill were happy to see those green sprouts in that black soil. They felt hopeful as those bean plants grew and grew and grew.

108

113

54C

Then Jack and Jill went down the hill to fetch a pail of water. Jack and Jill drenched the dry black soil one cupful at a time. Jack and Jill waited hopefully.

112

At last, Jack came back with a bagful of beans. Jack looked joyful. He felt hopeful, but Jill was still upset. Jack had traded his nice fat cow for that bagful of silly beans!

109

That bagful of beans could not feed them for long. Then Jill heard Jack's idea. Jill liked it a lot. She gladly helped Jack with his plan.

Jack and Jill quickly got spades and rakes. Jack and Jill dug up some rows on their plot of land. Jack and Jill planted Jack's beans in long rows.

110

111

Ruth's Day

by Brady Frances

illustrated by Hideko Takahashi

When Ruth got home, Mom gave her a big hug. Ruth felt so happy. She had a great day!

122

Buzz! The clock buzzed loudly.
Ruth slowly got out of bed.
Ruth stretched and yawned.
She was still sleepy.

115

Ruth sat with Edith. Edith smiled
sweetly. Ruth smiled back. It was
fun to sit with Edith. Ruth felt happy.

The bus stopped and beeped.
Ruth was just in time. She sat
behind the driver. Ruth had not
missed the bus. She felt happy.

118

119

Stew for Peg

by Frank Fenn

illustrated by Laurie Hamilton

"Thank you! Thank you all!"
squealed happy Peg. "What a
yummy stew this is!"

130

Jo Owl sat in her cozy home.
It was Peg Pig's birthday. Jo wanted
to make a treat for Peg.

123

"Peg likes stew," hooted Jo. "I will make a big pot of stew for Peg."

Jo was not able to make stew on her own. She didn't know how. She put a big pot of water in her cart. She went to ask for help.

124

Jo went to Peg's with her stew. "What a treat!" squealed Peg. "How did you make such yummy stew, Jo?"

"I had some help," hooted Jo.

129

62C

"Is it hot?" asked Hugo.

"Really yummy stew must be hot."

Hugo helped Jo heat it up.

"Thanks, Hugo!" hooted Jo.

"This stew smells yummy!"

128

Toby was helpful. He put a cupful of red stuff in the pot.

"This will make Peg's stew really yummy," Toby quacked loudly.

"Thanks, Toby!" hooted Jo.

125

63C

Lulu was helpful. She put a
handful of green leaves in the pot.
"This will make Peg's stew really
yummy," Lulu chattered quickly.
"Thanks, Lulu!" hooted Jo.

Jo went back home. Hugo
happened to be there.
"Hi," said Hugo. "What is in
that pot?"
"It's really yummy stew for Peg,"
hooted Jo.

126

127

64C

Amy Ant

by Denise Dinkleman

illustrated by Jon Goodell

Summer is ending. Winter will soon be on its way. Amy has to go back down into her home. She waves at Rupert. She is not sad. She will see him in the sunshine next spring!

138

Amy Ant wakes up. It has been a long, sleepy winter. Now winter is over. It is time to leave her cozy bed.

131

Amy makes her way up to the field. It is sunny. How good that sunshine feels! Spring has come at last.

"You're as brave as a tiger!" Amy tells him.

After that, Amy and Rupert meet every day. They take walks and look at flowers. They talk and have fun.

132

137

66C

Amy shouts for help. A flying
mantis hears her. He flies into the
flower and saves Amy!
Amy thanks him and thanks him!
He tells her that his name is Rupert.

136

Flowers are blooming. Amy
decides to pick some. She sniffs the
roses. She loves that smell the most.
It reminds her of sunny days.

133

When her backpack is full, Amy returns home. The sweet smell of roses fills each room. Amy is so happy she hums a tune. Soon music fills each room, too.

One day, Amy sees a blue flower. She did not see it before. She crawls up for a better look. Amy slips! Down, down, she slides. She is not able to get out.

134

135

68C

Julie and Jason

by Mason Sciele

illustrated by France Brassard

Julie spotted Jason by a big plant. She smiled. Jason saw Julie and hopped out. Julie was so happy! Her brothers were happy, too.

146

Julie has a pet rabbit named Jason. Jason has black and white fur. He sleeps in a cozy rabbit hutch on Julie's back porch. Julie got Jason when he was a baby.

139

Julie feeds Jason rabbit pellets and hay. Jason likes his dinner. He can sit up and behave like a dog. After he eats, Jason can behave like a cat. He curls up on Julie's lap.

140

No one was able to find Jason. Julie was sad. Then she had an idea. Was Jason playing "Hide and Seek"? She looked in places Jason had hidden before.

145

70C

Julie asked her brothers if they had seen Jason. Julie's brothers were sorry they had let Jason hop away. Then everyone looked for Jason outside.

144

Each day, Julie takes Jason out of his hutch. Jason likes to play "Hide and Seek." Jason hides and Julie seeks. Jason sits still and silent as Julie hunts for him.

141

71C

One day, Julie's brothers took Jason with them on a picnic. They did not see Jason hop off beyond the picnic table.

142

It was time for Julie to play with Jason. Jason was not in his hutch or on the porch. Julie looked all over the house. She even looked behind the drapes. Julie was upset. She couldn't believe Jason was missing!

143

72C

Home at Last

by Forest Von Gront
illustrated by Kristin Barr

The long day was over. There was still a lot to do, but it felt like home. Tony loved it! So did Mom and Dad.

154

Tony and his family were in their new home. Tony was happy. Everyone was happy!

147

73C

Dad repainted Tony's new bedroom. Tony helped. Dad let Tony decide which paint he liked. Tony was glad he chose blue.

148

Tony helped unpack dishes, pots, and pans. Dad set up a table. Mom, Dad, and Tony ate their first meal in their new home.

153

74C

Tony found his box of toys. Then his bedroom began to look like home. It was nice to settle in so quickly.

Dad unwrapped three new lights. He replaced the old lights. Tony's new room looked much brighter.

152

149

75C

Then the van came at noon.
The workers quickly unloaded the
van. Everyone helped put things
where they belonged.

Tony unpacked his books. He
and Mom unpacked sheets and
made his bed. Before long, the
room started to look cozy.

150

151

76C

Soccer

by Tia Yushi

illustrated by Linda Solovic

When the game ends, players say
"Good job!" no matter who wins.
Kids have fun replaying soccer games
by telling and retelling plays their
team made.

162

Many people believe soccer
is the best sport. Most boys and
girls play soccer.

155

Each player is dressed for soccer. This coach and everyone on his team have the same kind of shirt. This team chose red shirts with dots. This is the red team.

156

A goalkeeper is the only player who can pick up the ball. He or she can catch it and keep it out of the goal. Goalkeepers must react fast and stop goals.

161

Each team's job is to score goals.
Blue team players try to kick the ball
into the red team's goal. Each team
has a goalkeeper. The red team's
goalkeeper tries to stop the blue
team's players from making goals.

This coach and her team decided
on stripes. This is the blue team.
Their shirts look unlike the red team's
shirts. These players are putting on
long socks over shin pads.

160

157

79C

Soccer teams need good skills. At first, team players may be unskilled at using only their feet on the field. The more teams play, the more skillful players get.

Soccer is a fast game. Soccer teams must behave safely. It is unsafe and unkind to bump into players. It is a coach's job to teach and remind players to play safely.

158

159